A C[...]
YEARBOOK

festivals ☥ superstitions
traditional remedies ☥ folklore
herblore ☥ mead and soap making
elixirs ☥ legends ☥ recipes

LIZZY SHANNON

A PACIFIC NW LITERARY BOOK

an imprint of Sheffield Publications

A Celtic Yearbook

Editor - Leona Leigh Grieve

Interior Art – Lizzy Shannon

Cover Art © Jeff Sturgeon www.jeffsturgeon.com

Digital Photography - Paul Sprouse

ISBN-13: 978-0615539874

ISBN-10: 0615539874

Printed and bound in the United States.

A CELTIC YEARBOOK

LIZZY SHANNON

A PACIFIC NW LITERARY BOOK

an imprint of Sheffield Publications

DEDICATIONS

It goes without saying that this book is dedicated to my dear mother, Maureen Blythe, who passed away in October 2003.

But I'd also like to dedicate A Celtic Yearbook to another woman who has become a major influence in my life. She has been my friend and mentor since 2004. I wouldn't have written a word if not for her friendship and encouragement.

With grateful thanks to
Irene Radford

ACKNOWLEDGMENTS

Books don't get written without help and support from a great many people. I'd like to take this opportunity to thank the following for being encouraging, patient, kind, supporting and tolerant.

My father - Jim Blythe, Neil Shannon, Scott Simmons, Leona Leigh Grieve, Gwen Gades and Gabrielle Harbowy of Dragon Moon Press, Jeanette Cottrell, Bob Brown, Brenda Cooper, Jay Lake, Amy Carpenter of Book Universe, Ian Blythe, Carletta Blythe, Steve Blythe, Moya McCloskey, Mike McCloskey and in memory of his dear Kevin Jewitt, Fiona Blythe, Daniel Blythe, Clare Foster, Jenny Osborne, Terry McAuley, Edith Duncan, Jeff Sturgeon, Wendy Sue Reeve, Carrie McClanahan, Jessica Polanco, Jennifer Easton, Cathy Seguine, Lynne (Steane) Vinton, Jeff Fennel, Brenda and Paul Matera, Maggie MacDonald and Eric Gessner, Betty Acres, Joan Miller, June (Clark) Wilson, Barbara (Taggart) Nickels, Bill Johnson, Liam Collins, Joanne Gherke, Steve Ostrian, Heather McLaughlin, Patrick Wiese, Marilyn McGuire, Barbara Winter, Lynn de Beauclair, Melissa Winter, Melissa Welsh, and all the Sherwood Sisters of the Hearth, Trenna Landers, Bridgette Dever Storey, Gloria Chapman, Herbert Piekow, Magan Boyle, Jessie McClanahan, Duncan and Corwin Sturgeon, David and Sid Bodin, Danny Manus, Diana Portwood and Bob's Beach Books, and the Willamette Writers.

TABLE OF CONTENTS

A CELTIC YEARBOOK

A CELTIC YEARBOOK

FOREWARD

When Lizzy asked me to write her an introduction to this fascinating little book, I pointed out to her that I'm an odd choice. I'm about as Celtic as Prince Philip. Less so, truly, since my ancestry is pure, unadulterated *Sassenach*. In American terms, I'm as WASP as you can get, minus the trust fund. In Celtic terms, my personal heritage would make me about as popular in an Irish history class as a full blown case of the chicken pox.

Still, Lizzy and I have been friends for years, and I can't help but do something when she asks nicely. (Or naughtily, for that matter.) So I spent some time with *A Celtic Yearbook*. And I'm here to tell you, whatever your heritage; this little book is a great deal of fun.

It's not a narrative. It's not a how-to. I don't think this book will teach you very much about being Irish. But that's not the point. Lizzy's gone and collated the sayings and quirks she learned at her mother's knee in the Belfast of her childhood into an almanac of facts, stories, recipes and wisecracks that will keep you engaged and entertained through a sitting or two as well as throughout the year.

Want to know what a dropped fork means? She'll tell you. Want a recipe for a facial cream guaranteed to keep you beautiful as an ageless Irishwoman? This book has it. Too many freckles? Lizzy shows you just what to do about it. Though I have to ask what truly constitutes "too many" freckles.

My advice is not to pick this book up and read it front to back as if it were a story. There's a story here, to be sure, but it's told in mood and implication and the odd corners of Irish culture. Honor that spirit, and keep the book about the place, or the e-reader, and browse when the mood strikes and the moment permits. *A Celtic Yearbook* follows the rhythms of the Irish year. Follow them yourself, and let chance lead you on a journey of discovery that will amuse, delight and inform.

At least, that's what I'll be doing with it.

Enjoy, and *sláinte mhaith*.

Jay Lake
Portland, OR

Jay Lake lives in Portland, Oregon, where he works on numerous writing and editing projects. His 2011/2012 books are Endurance *and* Kalimpura *from Tor Books, and* Love in the Time of Metal and Flesh *from Prime Books. His short fiction appears regularly in literary and genre markets worldwide. Jay is a past winner of the John W. Campbell Award for Best New Writer, and a multiple nominee for the Hugo and World Fantasy Awards.*

INTRODUCTION

I was born and grew up in Belfast, Northern Ireland. Consequently, the schools I attended taught British and English history, and somehow I missed that I was Irish, too. My mother told me we lived in the capital, so as we only received English news on television, for many of my early years I thought we lived in London, England.

When I immigrated to the States I discovered how many people here love Ireland and her rich, diverse history. But their impression of Ireland bore no resemblance to the one I knew. So I embarked on a voyage of discovery. Like any good American I began to research my roots. My advantage was that I didn't have to go through a heritage site; my family was available right there and then. Slowly I unpeeled our British facade to find the hidden Celt beneath. Growing up during "The Troubles" in Northern Ireland had forced each side into our respective heritages. I wondered why we couldn't be of *both* British and Irish heritage? Not so controversial if you think about it.

My father's uncle, whom I'd met when I was a child and remembered as a mild, Winnie-the-Pooh-bear type of man with Al Capone-style spats and a cane, turned out to be Ernest Blythe, a member of the original Irish Volunteers, and an associate of Éamon de Valera, who spent the Easter Rising of 1916 in prison.

Then conversely on the other side, another uncle turned out to have been a member of the infamous Black and Tans a few years later. An equal opportunity family!

My mother and her two sisters proved to be a surprising fountain of knowledge in the traditions of Ireland, and who without a thought had used many of the remedies in this book on my brothers and me.

This book is predominantly Irish Celtic as I know it. The contents are the knowledge shared with me by my mother, Maureen. It's an homage to her, and if I'd had a daughter I'd have passed this knowledge on to her. So, instead, here is A Celtic Yearbook... for all of us over the world with Celt blood running through our veins. There are more of us than you think.

Cheers and Sláinte!

Lizzy Shannon, 2011

Mum (Maureen Frazer) 1939

THE CELTIC CALENDAR

Like the Native Americans, Celtic traditions were handed down through the generations by mother to daughter and father to son. According to Robert Graves' work, *The White Goddess*, Celtic priests divided the calendar into thirteen months based on the lunar cycle. In the *Gallic Wars*, Julius Caesar observed about the Druids: "They do not think it right to commit their teaching to writing," so even their doctrines and beliefs were handed down orally. The word *Druid* derives from Gaelic, meaning *knowing the oak tree*.

The Celts believed that trees had magical abilities, that they could heal, and that they had memories. The superstitious practice of *touch wood* or *knock on wood* for good luck, or to ward off a jinx for speaking too soon, dates back to these pagan beliefs concerning trees.

The Celts also believed the universe was symbolic of an ancient tree, whose roots were bound to the earth and whose branches reached to the heavens. Their lunar cycle, similar to astrology, was associated with different species of sacred trees. Tree spirits, known as Dryads, were believed to have distinct personalities and inhabited each of these sacred trees. Like the astrological signs, each lunar month was associated with a specific tree and personality traits of its Dryad. This Yearbook is divided into thirteen months, headed up by each sacred tree and its Dryadic trait. Which one are you?

The Celts measured the Solar year on a wheel,
which symbolizes creation and the constant
movement of the universe growth and
development.

⊤

BIRCH

BEITHE

December 24ᵗʰ – January 21ˢᵗ

The BIRCH tree is said to be the first tree to leaf after winter. The Druids consider the birch to represent loyalty, purity, renewal, and rebirth. If you are born under this sign you are resilient, patient, and determined. You may be reserved in showing affection, but you're good strategists and will not be deterred by obstacles.

The Celtic warrior god, LUGH, who is the inventor of all arts and crafts, rules this sign. He is also known as the God of fire and protector of the weak. His sacred symbol is a spear.

Your stone is predominantly PICTURE JASPER. This stone's elixir can be used for treating disorders of the skin. The stone itself can aid a healthy immune system and can help bring out suppressed grief and fear.

Your spirit animal, the WHITE STAG, represents high ideals and aspirations.

The SUN is your planetary ruler.

CUSTOMS AND GIFTS

To wish someone a Happy Holiday in Gaelic you'd say, "Nollaig Shona Duit!" *(NoLik Suna Ditch)*

Christmas Day in Ireland as I remember it growing up was almost entirely a religious festival. Most people attended church or chapel on Christmas morning, which was a lovely family occasion. My brothers and I found it very hard to pay attention when all we could think about was getting home and opening the presents under the tree.

The eleven days after Christmas used to be set aside for parties and a great amount of visiting, and then ended on the twelfth night: Epiphany.

A distinctive Irish feature of Christmas decorations was a large candle placed in the front, main window and lit on Christmas Eve. It was supposed to serve as a symbol of welcome to Mary and Joseph in memory of the night they sought shelter in vain on that first Christmas Eve, but the welcome can apply to anyone. The ceremony of lighting the candle was one of many simple ancient rituals, during which prayers were said for the departed. The candle should be lit by the youngest member of the family, and extinguished only by someone named *Mary.*

TRADITIONAL CELTIC GIFT IDEAS

My mother grew up during the Second World War, so she was a child of rationing and making do. I remember her showing me how to make these inexpensive hand-made gifts. Potpourris and Pomanders make wonderful and practical presents for just about anyone. To open a closet and smell a spicy pomander is a delight, and a bowl of potpourri will spread a delicate fragrance throughout your home.

Play around with these recipes and mix your own concoctions. Romantic as many of these recipes sound, they were originally developed to mask the filthy and foul conditions in which most people lived, and to ward off evil odors that were thought to cause disease. So don't drink them!

POMANDERS

These would have been a necessity rather than a luxury in the days before modern trash collection, when chamber pots were emptied from windows into the streets, and bathing considered to be dangerous. My father told me that his great uncle had believed that washing weakened the immune system and the body's ability to ward off disease.

To make a pomander, stick an orange full of cloves and roll it in orris powder. Another way is to knead herbs and spices into beeswax and roll it into balls about the size of a baseball. Tie a ribbon around them and hang in closets, bathrooms, or anywhere you'd like it to smell good.

POTPOURRIS

Dry flowers and herbs separately, then mix together. The powdered herbs or spices should be added last. When essential oils are used, mix them with a little of the orris powder until they are absorbed and then add to the potpourri. Keep the mixture for one month in a closed jar before using.

LAVENDER POTPOURRI
9 oz lavender flowers
1½ oz common salt
¾ oz dried thyme
¾ oz dried mint

¼ oz ground cloves
¼ oz ground caraway
Prepare as above.

APHRODISIAC POTPOURRI

Large dash bergamot essence
Large dash citrus medica
Dash lemon essence
Dash grains amber (*ambergris*)

Put all the ingredients into a bottle and pour in 8 cups strong spirits of wine. Keep the mixture tightly corked and shake it well two or three times a day for two weeks. Filter it through paper and put it into small bottles, then cork tightly. Remember, do not drink the mixture!

NEW YEAR TRADITIONS

With my mother's Scottish heritage, she infused *Hogmanay* into our New Year celebrations. The usual custom is for gunpowder to be fired at midnight, (not a good thing in Belfast!) so a couple of fireworks or sparklers did just fine. Then the merry-makers set out to *first foot* their neighbors' homes. It was considered good luck to have a dark-haired person cross the threshold first. To ensure their welcome, they brought a lump of coal, a black bun, and a bottle of good Scotch. The name Hogmanay is said to come from the Anglo-Saxon *Haleg Monath* (Holy Month), or the Gaelic *oge maidne* (New Morning).

Another traditional Hogmanay celebration is the *Creaming of the Well*. The cream referred to is the first water from the local well or spring on a New Year's Day. Single females would race to draw the first water, as they believed it guaranteed that she would be married within the new year. But for it to work, she had to get the man she desired to drink the water before midnight on that first day of the year.

Although Hogmanay is unique to Scotland, all Celtic lands have the same theme: The New Year must begin on a positive note, leaving negativity from the year before far behind. That's how the tradition of the New Year's Resolution was born.

⊤⊤

ROWAN

LUIS

January 22ⁿᵈ – February 18ᵗʰ
IMBOLC February 1st

The ROWAN (or mountain ash) tree is famed for having good protection against evil. It was commonly planted by doors and gates to ward off evil, and was thought to guard the gateway to the Other World. The rowan is also known as a fertility symbol. If you're born under this sign you like change, and scorn rules and convention. You are an original thinker, idealistic and artistic.

BRIGID, the Goddess of fertility and fire rules this sign. She represents the celestial mother, and is also known as the Goddess of learning, inspiration, agriculture and animal husbandry.

Your stone is predominantly the UNAKITE. This stone's elixir can be massaged into pressure points to promote clarity of thinking. The stone helps self-esteem and changes negative thinking to positive.

Your spirit animal is the DRAGON, giving you an imagination that knows no bounds.

Your planetary ruler is URANUS.

IMBOLC

This is the special day of Brigid, the Celtic goddess of fire. Flames can transform and signify change and the setting of new goals. The Crone of winter gives way to the Maiden of spring, nature starts to come back to life, and the new season begins.

St. Brigid has had countless miracles attributed to her. It is said that when her nursemaid was thirsty, Brigid transformed water into fine ale. When she was a little older, she was apparently cooking for her father's homecoming when a starving stray dog turned up at the kitchen door. She took pity on the animal and gave it her father's dinner, but when her father arrived, the food miraculously was restored to his plate. Brigid became the Abbess of Kildare, where she healed the blind, the mute, the insane, and those afflicted with leprosy. She is known as the patron saint of dairy workers because they say the cows she raised at Kildare produced a lake of milk every day. The St. Brigid's Cross is hung to this day in homes and barns to drive away evil.

ELIXIRS

Never drink these elixirs – add them to vegetable oil for massage or to burn as an essential oil, or pour into into your bath water. Only use glass containers/jars, and mineral water that has not been in contact with metal. Take the precious stone that you wish to use and put it in the glass jar, then pour the water over it. Leave the jar in the sun and moon for 24 hours to infuse it with astronomical energy.

Druids would take great care in preparing elixirs. They'd place the jar of water containing a precious stone in the sun on the first day of a full or new moon, and leave it for seven days so the energy from the moon would enhance the elixir. Then they would put the jar in a very dark place, surrounding it with seven of the same precious stone for another seven days. After fourteen days, they'd take an ounce of alcohol and mix it with the liquid to stabilize the energies. They called this the *Mother Elixir*, and stored it in a dark bottle in a dark place until they needed it.

SOME UNUSUAL CURES

Don't try these at home! My mother just thought these were amusing and jotted them down in her notebook. I do remember an elderly man who lived not far from my parents in The Spa, County Down. He created charms like the one mentioned here for ague. We never knew what he put in the bag, but when one of our neighbors had shingles she swears that the charm cured her. The man never took payment, but would only accept tea or cookies in exchange for his services.

To cure an EYELID STYE, rub a gold wedding ring across it, point a gooseberry thorn at it nine times saying, "Away, away, away!" or stand at a crossroads and recite, "Stye, stye, leave my eye... take the next one coming by!"

To banish WARTS, find a funeral, take some of the clay from under the feet of the men who bear the coffin and apply it to the wart. Wish strongly while applying that it may disappear.

To cure a TOOTHACHE, carry close to your body the two jaw bones of a haddock. Ever since the miracle of the loaves and fishes these bones are an infallible remedy against toothache. The older they are the better.

To enhance VIRILITY take two ounces of cochineal, one ounce of gentian root, two pinches of saffron, two pinches of snakeroot, two pinches of salt of wormwood, and the rind of ten oranges. Steep in a quart of brandy and use when needed.

To find WEALTH, take a rooster's heart, and after nightfall go to the center of a crossroads. Holding some money in your hand all the while, throw the heart over your left shoulder in the name of the cockerel. Ever after, no matter what you spend you will always find the same piece of money undiminished in your pocket.

To ease a STITCH IN THE SIDE, rub unsalted butter into the affected side and make an 'x' sign seven times over it.

To become INVISIBLE, take a raven's heart and split it open. Make three cuts and place a black bean in each. Then plant it and when the beans sprout, put one in your mouth and incant, "By virtue of this bird's heart and by strength of its great art, I desire to be invisible." So it will be as long as the bean is kept in the mouth. (I think my mother must have used this frequently, the amount of times she seemed to appear from nowhere when I was doing something I shouldn't!)

To cure MUMPS, wrap the child in a blanket and go to a pigsty. Rub the child's head on the back of a pig, and the mumps will leave the child and pass into the animal.

For AGUE, a few spiders tied up in a bag and worn around the neck will keep off fever, but no-one except the faery doctor must ever open the bag or the charm will be broken.

To cure FEVER, place the patient on the sandy shore when the tide is coming in, and the retreating waves will carry away the disease.

⊤⊤⊤

ASH

NUINN

February 19th – March 18th

ASH trees are more prone to being struck by lightning than any other tree, so the druids considered it enchanted. Its wood was carved into wands and spears, and the tree itself was considered to represent the link between all the heavens and earth. If you're born under this sign you are intelligent, quick witted, curious and creative.

GWYDION, storyteller and magician, rules this sign. He is known as a master of illusion and Druid of the Gods.

Your stone is both the UNAKITE as described in Rowan, but as complicated as you are born under the ASH, you are also the AMETHYST. This is a stone of transformation and purity. Dab the elixir of the amethyst on your body if you want to be in tune with all thing spiritual, psychic and mystic. It brings calmness to a troubled heart.

Your animal spirit is the ADDER, which represents spiritual energy and enlightenment.

Your planet is NEPTUNE.

SAINT PATRICK

If you love anything Celtic, then you have heard the legend of St. Patrick casting the snakes out of Ireland. Around the year 406, raiders from Ireland attacked English shores and took captives as slaves, Patrick amongst them. He was put to work as a shepherd, alone and in very poor living conditions. In his despair he turned to prayer, asking God to free him. When his prayers were answered and he escaped back to England, in gratitude he traveled to France to study for the priesthood.

After his ordination he claimed he had a dream in which he heard the voices of millions of Irish crying, "Come back, young man, and walk among us once again!"

He returned to Ireland as a missionary bishop and devoted the rest of his life to preaching Christianity to the Irish.

As for the snakes, well... there are none to be found in Ireland today, so who can say?

WARRIOR'S HAIR

Hair-restorers have always been important throughout the ages. In St. Patrick's time, the amount of hair a man sported was an indication of his prowess as a hunter or lover. However, some of the old recipes might kill the user rather than cure the loss of hair, with ingredients such as bear grease, ashes of bees, and mouse or goat's dung!

My mother used all the following recipes throughout her life, on herself and on me and my brothers. So far, all of us still sport a pretty good head of hair. (So far, so good, anyway.)

The recipes included here are based solely in alcohol. In most cases they have to stand for several days and then be filtered. A coffee filter is ideal for this purpose, but some lotions will have to be filtered several times until the liquid is completely clear.

Putting too much alcohol-based concoctions on the scalp might cause it to become dry and flaky, so use occasionally. Gently rub the lotions into the hair with your fingers, using a circular massage movement. And as I keep reminding you, do not drink any of these!

FOR THINNING HAIR
3½ oz alcohol
3½ oz scent
1 oz rum
1¼ oz castor oil
1¼ oz Peruvian bark

Steep the Peruvian bark in alcohol for 3 days. Sieve. Add to the other ingredients.

TO STIMULATE GROWTH
2 oz alcohol
Dash Peruvian balsam
Dash rosemary tincture
Dash orange blossom water
Dash tincture of Peruvian bark

FOR SENSITIVE SKIN
2 oz alcohol
1 drop Peruvian balsam
1 oz distilled water
2 drops rosemary oil
¼ oz arnica tincture

CHAMOMILE LOTION
FOR BLONDE HAIR
2 grams alcohol
¾ oz chamomile tincture
¼ oz St. John's Wort tincture
I oz rosewater

For RED and DARK hair, substitute rosemary instead of chamomile.

FRESH NETTLE LOTION
Nettles are excellent for stimulating the circulation of the scalp and improving hair condition. Take one part of fresh stinging nettles to three parts alcohol. Let the mixture stand for two weeks in the sun. Filter carefully. Use three teaspoons of this tincture to 9 oz water.

NETTLE TINCTURE LOTION
2 oz alcohol
¾ oz nettle tincture
I drop Peruvian balsam
I oz orange blossom water
Few drops lavender oil

BIRCH ANTISEPTIC HAIR LOTION
2 oz alcohol
I oz birch leaf tincture
I oz birch bud tincture
¾ oz water

This is very effective in conditioning hair and stimulating growth. Rosemary or lavender oil added will give it a pleasant scent.

HAIR RINSES

The following rinses are mostly simple herbal infusions or decoctions. They are not as strong as the hair tonics and are used more as a preventative to keep the hair in good condition.

Lime flower is one of the best infusions to maintain soft and shining hair. An infusion of birch leaves or buds will have the same effect. Birch sap is also good for conditioning. It can be collected in early Spring by making a deep cut in the tree trunk when the sap will run out slowly and can be caught in a bowl. A spoonful of this in the last rinse water will effectively strengthen and protect your hair from the elements.

Rosemary decoction makes an effective and pleasantly scented rinse for dark or red hair. Simmer a small bunch of fresh rosemary (or two tablespoons dried) for ½ hour in ½ liter water. Chamomile infusion can be used for blonde, gray, or white hair.

Arnica can help prevent dandruff and stimulate the circulation in the scalp. Infusions of rose, jasmine, violet and lavender will impart a lasting fragrance to your hair, which makes the use of commercial perfumes completely unnecessary.

Beer, at the risk of making you smell like a brewery, is the simplest and most effective way of giving body to your hair, and makes a great setting lotion.

Before washing your hair, give your scalp a wet massage to stimulate hair growth. Dampen your hair and beginning at the nape of your head, knead your scalp with the fingertips, keeping the fingers well spread. Repeat this process beginning from the temples and forehead and working to the back of the head.

Dry hair can be greatly improved by massaging this way using almond oil. After massaging the oil into the head, wrap a warm towel around your hair to increase the absorption. Wash your hair thoroughly after 20 minutes. The same treatment will successfully clear up dandruff.

Olive oil is another anti-dandruff treatment, which is used for fine, easily damaged, and difficult to manage hair. It is best to give your hair an intensive treatment with olive oil so that as much of it as possible is absorbed. Apply it in the same way as the almond oil but try to leave it on for at least 6 hours, or overnight. Wash out the oil thoroughly in the morning and your hair will be left shining and manageable.

Only try this when you have some time alone! Rub your scalp with a clove of garlic. It's very good for the hair and a well-known treatment to prevent hair loss and increase blood circulation in the scalp. It is a strong antiseptic and a useful anti-Seborrhea treatment. The smell may put you off but a good herbal shampoo will wash away the smell. Onion can be used in the same way as garlic but is considerably milder. You can also rinse your hair with onion decoction. The smell is then still present but is less penetrating. Egg yolk is another good conditioner and smells less obnoxious. Take one lightly beaten egg yolk and rub this into your damp hair. Leave it on for 10 minutes and then rinse with lukewarm water.

You can treat oily hair by adding 1 teaspoon natural sea salt to every 2 oz of shampoo. Do not use hot water to wash your hair. Although there will not be much lather your hair will still be clean.

The addition of lemon juice to the last rinse water will also help to keep the hair less oily and give it a lovely shine. But be warned, it will bleach the hair slightly. One summer I ended up looking like a faded canary from using too much lemon juice.

HERBAL SHAMPOO
1 handful birch buds and leaves
1 teaspoon fresh birch juice
1 handful fresh nettles
4 cups water
5½ oz grated castile soap (made from olive oil)

Prepare an infusion using two to three tablespoons of fresh herb (or one tablespoon dried herb) to the distilled water. Sieve and add 5 ½ oz grated castile soap and bring the mixture slowly to the boil, stirring all the time until the water is clear. Remove from the heat and beat the mixture until it is fluffy. Pour into a jar.

ᚋ

ALDER

FEARN

March 19th – April 15th
VERNAL EQUINOX March 21st

The ALDER tree is said to be strong-hearted and determined. The wood is hardy and more resistant to rotting in water than other trees, so was used widely in building. If you're born under this sign you are self-reliant, adventurous, loving, and tenacious.

The God of the spirit world, BRAN THE BLESSED, rules this sign. His name means *raven*. He is a giant, and known as the God of Prophecy.

Your stone is PEACH AVENTURINE. Massage the elixir of this stone into muscles to help heal damage. This stone infuses energy and helps with rejuvenation when tired. It will aid in clarity of thought when making decisions.

Your spirit animal is the FOX, which represents skill in diplomacy.

MARS is your planetary ruler.

HEALING AND RENEWAL

Celtic healers have known the secrets of herbal remedies for centuries. My mother used a lot of these remedies and she never looked her true age. The following recipes date back to the Middle Ages and have been passed down from generation to generation since King Conchubar ruled in Emain Macha, the ancient capital of Ulster.

Legend says if you gather herbs when the moon is waning, their magic properties will be more potent, for the wee folk will be nearby to bless them. It's a fun thought, but the truth is there'll be less sap in the herbs' leaves and they'll dry better. Whether gathered by moonlight or in the noonday sun, drying them is simple. Either spread them out on paper, covered by a piece of muslin or hang them up in bunches, heads downward.

Today, almost every single herb can readily be bought in stores, but it's a lot more fun to plant and grow your own. Most herbal plants are so easy to care for, it doesn't matter if you live on a farm or in an apartment building; you can grow them in window boxes, if necessary.

Your herbs should be stored in airtight cans or jars, (produce canning jars are perfect) and remember to protect them from the light. This way they should stay fresh for about a year.

Before their cosmetic use was discovered, herbs were simmered in lard or butter to make medical ointments. Butter still makes an acceptable natural face cream for very dry skin, but lard enlarges the pores, and is too greasy to make a pleasant base for cosmetics. The recipes in this book are all easy to prepare and require no complicated implements. If you want to do it the old-fashioned way, use a pestle and mortar. You can use a blender as it saves so much time, but the very act of pummeling your ingredients in the old way can be therapeutic.

When adding the watery ingredients, do it drop by drop to the oils and fats so that they can be absorbed, otherwise you'll end up with a greasy mess. Use distilled water rather than water from the faucet. Bottled mineral water works perfectly. All the measures listed are approximate. Experiment with them as you gain experience. For example, you'll soon learn to adjust the texture of your creams by using a few flakes of white wax. Exchange different fragrances to suit your moods. If you perfect your recipes, they make marvelous, personalized gifts.

Here are five simple methods for preparing herbs for use:

DECOCTION FOR
ROOTS AND BARKS
Boil the herbs for about 15 minutes. Then use a sieve to separate the herbs from the water. (A European coffee plunger works very well for this.)

INFUSION FOR
PLANTS AND LEAVES
Pour boiling distilled water over the herb and let it soak for about 5 minutes. Then sieve.

COLD INFUSION
FOR HERBAL VINEGAR
Steep the herb for several hours in cold liquid in a hermetically sealed airtight jar.

TINCTURE
Pound 3 ½ ounces of dried herb into a powder. Add 4 cups of medicinal alcohol, and store in a screw-top jar at room temperature. Shake the jar daily, and remember to filter the tincture before use.

ESSENTIAL OIL

Use ¼ cup of fresh, crushed herbs to 2 cups of vegetable (almond or sunflower) oil. Add I tablespoon of white wine vinegar. Pour the mixture into a screw-topped jar and shake. Keep in a warm, light place and let the oil mature for a month. Then strain and decant into a bottle.

BODY TREATMENTS

Some of these body packs and baths were originated to draw out disease or evil spirits. Today, they can tone up your skin, relax or invigorate, and make you feel fabulous.

Oatmeal is the most effective body pack. It removes impurities from the skin and improves tone and texture. Mix it into a fine paste with water, or even better, buttermilk, and smear it over your body. Sit on an absorbent towel and leave the pack on for about 15 minutes. Wash off with lukewarm water.

Lemon juice makes an astringent body pack, which sluices away dead cells and improves skin texture. Mix the juice with oatmeal or prepare a decoction of washed sliced whole lemons and oranges (including skins). Slice 2 lemons and 2 oranges, or 4 lemons and simmer these in 8 cups of water for ½ hour. Cool, sieve, and then use a sponge to spread the mixture over your body.

For a milk bath treatment, Cleopatra's favorite, mix 4 cups of milk with the juice of 2 lemons. Sponge over the body and leave on for 10 - 15 minutes. If your skin is really oily, or if you'd just like to cool down on a humid day, beat 4 eggs with juice of 4 lemons, then spread over your body. It is sticky to use, but very effective.

Bathing in general for many centuries was considered dangerous as too much water might weaken the constitution and encourage sickness. Herbal baths were rarely done to cleanse the body but used as cures.

Rosemary and lavender were the two most popular bathing herbs. A strong decoction of either of these will impart a heady and effective elixir to the bath water. Lavender is a natural disinfectant and also softens the skin. Today, the scent is associated with gentleness and serenity, but in the old days it was used in Ireland to strengthen the nerves of warriors prior to battle. Rosemary stimulates the circulation, peppermint infusion is invigorating, and chamomile is soothing. Geranium oil is best used at certain times of month, to soothe hormonal changes. Bathing in a light infusion of sage and geranium oil can help post-natal blues. If you have trouble getting to sleep, try a bath with some lavender and a little valerian root decoction before going to bed. The lavender will mask its unpleasant odor. Valerian root is used as a natural sleep aid in capsule form today.

The properties of St. John's Wort to aid depression has come into vogue in recent years, but the ancient Celtic healers have always known its power. Bathing in a St. John's Wort infusion is guaranteed to lift the spirits and place a better perspective on things.

Natural deodorant baths are great in the hot summertime. The Celts carried oakleaf or lovage in little bags to combat bad body odors. Use these as infusions in the bath water to keep you fragrant. To heal small scratches and abrasions on the skin, make horsetail into a decoction and add it to the bath water.

To soften skin, rose petals or honeysuckle leaves and flowers are best. If you have dry or chapped skin add a few drops of almond or sunflower oil.

There are so many different recipes you can concoct. Exploring with the following and experimenting with different ingredients should help you find the baths that work best for you.

17TH CENTURY HERBAL BATH
Brandy (for preservation)
Rosemary
Lavender

Thyme
Bay leaves
Peppermint
Wormwood
Lemon balm

Take a handful of each of these fresh herbs, or I tablespoon if dried, and boil them for 10 minutes in 8 cups water. Sieve the mixture and add ½ bottle brandy. Pour a little of this into your bath. The brandy acts as a preservative, so this mixture can be kept indefinitely.

LAVENDER BATH EXTRACT
3¼ oz distilled water
a dash of lavender oil
1¼ oz rosewater
I oz orange blossom water
2 cups brandy
3 handfuls lavender flowers

Pour the brandy over the fresh lavender flowers and leave it to stand for 3 days. Sieve carefully. Add the lavender oil, orange blossom water, rosewater and distilled water. Shake well and keep in an airtight bottle.

PINE BATH
Boil fresh pine needles and cones with five times their volume of water. Simmer for 40 minutes then press out all the liquid into a saucepan. Reduce this by

boiling until it thickens. Add 5½ oz extract to one bath. This is great for stimulating the circulation.

HERBAL BATH OIL
a dash essential oil of lavender,
a dash essential oil of thyme,
a dash essential oil of marjoram
I glass brandy

Shake the oils together in the brandy and add a teaspoonful of this mixture to your bath. The brandy prevents the mixture from clogging.

ᚈᚈᚈᚈ

WILLOW

SAILLE

April 16th – May 13th
BELTANE May 1st

The WILLOW is considered reliable and practical, able to bend and adapt to life's changes. If you're born under this sign you will be emotional and resourceful, and forget very little, as you possess an unfailing memory. The Willow was sacred to the Moon and in Celtic myth the universe was hatched from two eggs hidden among the boughs of the Willow.

The Celtic Moon Goddess, CERIDWEN, rules this sign. She is also known as the goddess of dark prophetic powers, and her symbol is a white sow.

Your stone is the SERPENTINE. This stone's elixir can be used to massage onto infected areas to rid your body of infection. The serpentine can help heal emotional and mental imbalances.

Your spirit animal, the HARE, represents adaptation and intuition.

The MOON is your planetary ruler.

BREWING YOUR OWN HONEY MEAD

The making of mead, or honey wine, is as traditional as the making of herbal remedies. Indeed, this particular kind of brew is probably one of the most ancient known to humankind, yet as enjoyable today as it has been for thousands of years.

Ingredients:
Dark honey
Distilled or spring water
Yeast (Montrachet wine yeast)

Lemons and tea are used to balance the brew and aid fermentation and flavor. It can take up to a year before it's ready to drink. If you'd like the mead ready in about four months, substitute Malic acid, citric acid, or grape tannin.

Use a clean gallon jug for each batch of mead. After pitching, you should allow at least four months before bottling, depending on how the fermentation goes. While the fermentation process takes place, the mead will get very cloudy.

Once it's bottled, let the mead age for at least another three months. Store the bottles somewhere where they can be left undisturbed at a temperature of 55 to 85 degrees Fahrenheit.

Equipment:
One-gallon jug
Clear glass primary fermenter, 6 quart
Brewing pot, 4 to 6 quarts
(steel or enamel, not aluminum)
Fermentation lock and stopper
Wire mesh tea strainer
Long-handled plastic brewing spoon
Racking cane
Plastic siphon hose, about 3 feet long
Bottle brushes, assorted
Bottles (recycled wine bottles are suitable)
Funnel, plastic
Corks for bottles
Bottle capper/cork compressor
Sulfite tablets if desired to terminate fermentation before final bottling.

The brew should be cooled in a primary fermenter before pitching the yeast. With a glass primary fermenter, it is possible to siphon the clear mead off from the sediment before you pitch the yeast. When you transfer the mead from one container to another, always use a siphon to avoid aerating the mead and exposing it to airborne bacteria.

A racking cane has a cap on the tip and a hole about an inch from the end. When you attach the siphon tube you can draw off the mead from the spent yeast and other sediment without stirring up sediment. Cut the racking cane down for use with a gallon jug.

BASIC MEAD RECIPE

2 quarts water
2½ lbs honey
I packet mead yeast
about ½ cup lemon peel or 3 teaspoons of Malic acid
I tablespoon strong tea or I½ teaspoons tartaric acid
¼ teaspoon grape tannin
I teaspoon yeast energizer

Stir the honey and water together, heating slowly. Stir in the lemon peel and tea (or the Malic and tartaric acid). When it gets hot, stir in the grape tannin and the yeast energizer. Use the tea strainer to skim off the froth that rises to the top. Let it cool, then *rack* or pour into your primary fermenter and let the brew cool overnight. Then carefully pour it through the strainer into the gallon fermentation jug. *Pitch* or add the yeast, stirring a packet of yeast into four ounces of 80-degree water. Let it sit for about ten minutes and stir it into the brew. Carefully move the jug to a dark, moderate-temperature place where it will be completely undisturbed, and put on the fermentation lock. After a few days the mead will start to clear, and there will be a good bit of sediment at the bottom of the jug. Pour the mead into another jug, being careful to leave the sediment behind. Then top off the jug with distilled or purified water, and re-attach the fermentation lock. If after a week or two the mead again has sediment, rack it again into another bottle. It's a good idea to check monthly for sediment, and re-rack if there's more than just a trace. When your mead has gone for a month without sediment, it's ready to be bottled and corked. This is where the sulfite tablet should be added to terminate any residual fermentation. Crush it and dissolve into two ounces of water, then stir into the gallon of mead. After allowing the mead to set overnight, funnel it into the bottles and cork. Let your mead age for three months or more.

A FEW NATURAL CURES

SORE THROAT

Prepare a hot drink by mixing equal parts lemon juice and tea, and sweeten with honey. Keep hydrating yourself with this until you feel better. Gargle periodically with warm salted water, and swallow some crushed ice in between. Wrapping a warm towel around your neck can further help relieve a sore throat.

HEADACHES

Put your thumbs in the center of each temple and massage firmly for a couple of minutes in a circular motion. Wrap a warm towel around your neck as sometimes tension from the neck can cause a headache. If it's a migraine, use ice on the area, as it will help shrink the blood vessels. Try taking the herb, *Feverfew*, as it has anti-inflammatory properties. Sometimes low blood sugar can cause headaches, so try eating a piece of fruit.

STINGS

Put ice on the sting to control swelling. Don't leave it on for any more than a few minutes each time. Make up a paste from baking soda and apply to the area. If the site is itchy, apply a compress from a washcloth soaked in cool water. Elevate the area if the site aches.

For nettle stings, look around for Dock Leaves, and rub on the area. My father says, "Docken in; nettle out." I remember using them in the woods when I was a child to take the pain away from nettle stings. They worked pretty well.

CUTS AND SCRAPES

Apply pressure to the area until bleeding stops. Wash the area with soap and water and rinse under running water until the area is completely clean. If adhesive bandages are not immediately available, a cobweb will help seal the area and keep the edge of the cut together.

BURNS

Immediately run cold water over the area. If no water is available, milk will work. Apply a washcloth soaked in cool water (do not use ice). Clean the burn area twice a day with mild soap and water. Keep hydrated to help expedite healing, and moisturize the area daily.

RASHES

Soak a washcloth in cool water and oatmeal and put over the rash for about ten minutes. Try a compress of milk and water, making sure to rinse thoroughly afterward. Or make a paste from baking soda and water and dab that on the area. Witch hazel can be most effective in cooling irritated skin. I used to apply it as a toner after removing my makeup, as I have very sensitive skin, which reddens easily.

⊥

HAWTHORNE

HUATH

May 14th – June 10th

The HAWTHORN tree, with its sharp thorns, used to be wielded as psychic protection against evil spirits. If you're born under this sign, you are charming and creative, usually in the performance field. You need challenges to feel fulfilled or you become quickly bored.

The summer flower maiden, OLWEN, rules this sign. Her name means *white footprint;* it's said that white lilies sprout wherever she walks.

Your stone is the GREEN AVENTURINE. This stone's elixir is excellent to massage into your body for stimulating muscle tissue. This is a healing stone, and helps release fear and anxiety. It will aid you in times of turmoil and change.

Your spirit animal is the OWL, which represents wisdom and patience.

VULCAN is your planetary ruler.

PURIFICATION FOR THE BODY

Beltane is celebrated on May 1st. It's focus is on fertility, when the earth mother opens up to the fertility god, and their union is expected to bring abundant crops and healthy livestock. It's a time to think about new life, and many people begin spring cleaning around this time of year. What better time than to think about spring cleaning your metabolism, which will be sluggish after the long, cold months.

Start by drinking eight 8oz glasses of water a day, which works like a miracle to cleanse your system. Make the first glass of the day before breakfast a warm glass of water.

Add herbs to your drinking water to create a *depurative* to help purify the system. Choose from watercress, burdock, nettles, plantain, birch leaves, or borage. Fresh nettles can be cooked and eaten like spinach (itself a good depurative) or used in soups.

Birch leaf tea is a particularly efficient purifying beverage. Add it to your warm water first thing in the morning. Also try dried burdock root decoction: 1½ - 3 oz to 4 cups of water. Drink a glass of this after every meal. It can also be used externally as a lotion.

DEPURATIVE TEA
½ oz sage
¾ oz raspberry leaves
¾ oz hawthorn leaves

Boil 5 tablespoons of this herbal mixture in 4 cups of water. Let it reduce to about 3 cups. Drink once daily.

PURIFYING JUICE
Borage
Watercress
Dandelion

Take equal quantities of these herbs and extract the juice in a blender. Take a teaspoonful twice daily. Keep in the freezer.

If your skin breaks out during your purification, try this astringent lotion. Note, if you have sensitive skin, use witch hazel instead.

ASTRINGENT LOTION
I oz alcohol
¼ oz rosewater
¼ oz lemon oil

2 drops bergamot

Shake the ingredients together and apply twice daily.

FRECKLES AND BLOTCHES

Freckles, the scourge of the Irish red-head! The best way to prevent them is to stay out of the sun, but there are ways to lighten them. Rinsing with an infusion of lime flowers, primrose flowers or rosemary can lighten the skin and slough off the dullness of winter. Lemon parsley juice works well, too. In old times, buttermilk was used to lighten the skin.

Make a compress with squashed tomatoes or aubergine juice and apply to the face to bleach away freckles, or try cucumber and lemon juice.

For noticeable birthmarks or blemishes on the body, try fresh horseradish. (Note: do not use horseradish on the face!) Grate the horseradish finely and pound it into a pulp, soften with a little lemon juice and smooth over the mark.

LIGHTENING CREAM
I egg white
7 oz distilled water
½ oz icing sugar
Juice of I lemon

Beat the egg white until stiff and add the other ingredients gradually, beating all the time. Massage this mixture into your skin before sleeping.

LIGHTENING BODY CREAM
2 cups wine vinegar
1 horseradish root finely grated

Put this mixture in a bottle. Seal it well and stand it in the sun for two days. Use this before going to bed. The added advantage is that the smell will act as a natural bug guard!

IRISH WRITERS AND ARTISTS
-CONNECTIONS

Seamus Heaney, 1939-
Mr. Heaney lived next door to Mum's sister, Auntie Joan, just north of Belfast. He was born in the city known to locals as Stroke City (Derry or Londonderry). He encouraged all of us to write, and indeed may have been responsible for me writing today. My aunt had some poems published in a local magazine in Northern Ireland, thanks to his influence. Of all his work, my favorite poem remains *Blackberry Picking*. I'll never forget these words that seemed to capture the very essence: *"You ate that first one and its*

flesh was sweet Like thickened wine: summer's blood was in it."

Oscar Wilde, 1854-1900
Dublin born Wilde's most famous works include *The Picture of Dorian Gray, Lady Windermere's Fan, A Woman of No Importance, An Ideal Husband,* and *The Importance of Being Earnest.* I was in a production of *Earnest* in London, and played the infamous Lady Bracknell.

As Lady Bracknell

George Bernard Shaw, 1856-1950
Shaw was born in Dublin. At age 70 he received the Nobel Prize for his play, *Saint Joan.* His other famous works include *Candida, The Man of Destiny, Arms and the Man, Pygmalion,* and *You Never Can Tell.* I performed in two of his plays for the Shaw Society in Shaw's Corner in Ayot St. Lawrence in England. Below

is a photograph of me as Catherine Petkoff in a London production of *Arms and the Man.*

As Catherine Petkoff

James Galway, 1939-
Mr. Galway was Mum's favorite modern-day musician. He was born in Belfast and rose to become the most famous flautist in Ireland. We went to watch him play many times over the years. I remember one particular concert when he paused between bars to take a breath, one enthusiastic member of the audience broke out into loud applause. Realizing he was the only one, his face flushed beet red. Mr. Galway lowered his flute, bowed to him and said, "Thank you very much," making everyone laugh and rescuing the man from his embarrassment.

OAK

DUIR

June 11th – July 8th
SUMMER SOLSTICE June 21st

The OAK tree was the most sacred of all to the Druids. It was another wood that warded off evil spirits, and people began making their doors out of oak. If you're born under this sign you are intelligent and patient, able to learn quickly and accumulate wisdom. You're a born leader, and are steadfast and true. You are not easily swayed by opposition.

The Father of all Gods, the DAGDA, rules this sign. He is a master of magic, a fearsome warrior and a skilled craftsman.

Your stone is the QUARTZ. This stone's elixir can be applied directly onto burns and blisters to heal them. This stone is a great aid in focusing energy and giving you clarity of thought.

Your spirit animal is the WREN, the Celtic king of the birds, which represents intelligence and tact.

JUPITER is your planetary ruler.

LOVE

In Ireland, the month of June seems to host more weddings than at any other time of year. Here is the history of the Claddagh, the traditional Irish wedding ring. Claddagh is a tiny Galway fishing village, where the ring originated from. Legend says that the town designed a sigil to place on the sails of ships, and to be worn by the Sailors of Claddagh. When these sailors met other fishermen on their waters, if they did not see the Claddagh sigil, they would kill them.

The Claddagh is a heart held between a pair of hands with a crown above. The saying goes: "You are the queen/king of my heart; the heart I give to you".

Today, the ring is worn extensively in Ireland, either on the right hand with the heart pointed outwards showing that the wearer is free or with the heart turned inwards to denote that he or she is unavailable. The best place is on the left hand with the heart pointing inwards, showing that the wearer is happily and faithfully attached.

The Claddagh ring was developed by Richard Joyce, native of Galway. While being transported to the plantations of the Moorish West Indies as a slave, he was captured by pirates in the Mediterranean and trained in his craft by a goldsmith who bought him. He was set free in 1689, and he returned to Galway to make his famous Claddagh rings.

A more fanciful tale is that in the 1500's, a lady called Margaret Joyce married Domingo de Rona, a wealthy merchant from Spain. When he died, she shared his wealth with the poor. Apparently, Providence rewarded her for her generosity. She was sitting in the sun one day when an eagle flew over and dropped a gold ring into her lap. This was said to be the first Claddagh, and all others replicas of this celestial gift.

MARRIAGE

The ancient marriage ceremony was very simple. The couple merely declared before their families and friends that they were man and wife. Oftentimes the ceremony took place by standing stones, and if the stone had an aperture in it, the bride and groom would take each others' hands through it and declare themselves married. In Scotland this was known as *hand-fasting.*

LOVE POTIONS

My mother, (whom I assure you was happily married for over 50 years!) had jokingly noted down this love potion in her notebook. They were apparently taken from a book on Druidic practices.

Brew this tea on a Friday during a waxing moon to make another person fall in love with you.

1 pinch rosemary
2 teaspoons breakfast tea
3 pinches nutmeg
3 pinches thyme
3 fresh mint leaves
6 lemon leaves
6 fresh rose petals
3 cups spring water
Honey and sugar to taste

Put all ingredients into a tea kettle. Boil the spring water and pour over, adding honey and sugar to taste.

Recite the following before drinking:

"By light of moon waxing I brew this tea, to make (say the name of the person you want to love you) desire me."

Drink some tea and recite:

"Goddess of love, hear now my plea. Let (person's name) desire me. So mote it be. So mote it be."

On the following Friday brew a second pot of the love potion and give a cup to the person you named in the rhyme. Watch and see what happens!

DREAMS

To dream of love means you are longing for love. It's a desire to be able to love as well as to be loved. Think carefully about your emotions in the dream. If you dream you are falling in love it means someone loves you, and is about to tell you. If love passes you by in the dream, it means you'll soon be wed.

To dream of a wedding means you long for a permanent relationship and security. It spells happiness, although brief. If you are male and see yourself as the best man, you will find happiness in love. If you're female and see a best man, you'll have security and happiness.

To see a bride at the altar means great happiness in your life, but to see a bridegroom means delays in something you desire.

To see yourself as a bridesmaid portends disappointment. However, if you see several bridemaids, that means happiness is on the horizon.

If you dream you're in a relationship and see yourself admired, you may lose friends due to your own vanity. Admiring others means unhappiness.

If you elope in your dream, you and your partner could be facing a break up.

To dream that you are jilted means your lover will be faithful and constant.

||||

HOLLY

TEINN

July 9th – August 5th
LUGNASA August 1st

The HOLLY tree is considered to be a protector, its sharp points repelling enemies. A holly wreath on the door provides visual protection. If you're born under this sign you are logical, practical, and cautious. You have good business sense, and are steadfast in adversity. You are possessive and loving, and fast-acting.

The Smith God, GOVANNON, rules this sign. Those who drink from his sacred cup need no longer fear old age and infirmity.

Your stone is the AGATE. This stone's elixir can be massaged into muscles to help tone them. This stone brings balance and blocks negative energy.

Your animal spirit is the UNICORN, which represents strength and courage.

EARTH is your planetary ruler.

LUGNASA

This is an agrarian harvest festival, said to have been created by the god, Lugh, as a funeral feast and games celebration to commemorate his foster-mother, Tailtiu. She was said to have died of exhaustion after clearing the wild plains of Ireland for agriculture. It was known as the *Aenach Tailteann,* and was a favorite place for hand-fasting ceremonies as well as contests of skill and strength.

MAKING HOMEMADE SOAP

When making your own soap, please try to prepare it in a fully ventilated area or outside, as it's harmful to inhale lye. Things you'll need:

Lye

Lard

Oatmeal or grain (for texture if required)

Candy thermometer
Soap mold
Soap coloring
Coconut oil
Distilled or mineral water
Scented essential oils
Olive oil (not virgin)
Absorbent towels
Vinegar
Rubber Gloves
Measuring cups and spoons
Mixing spoons and bowls, including stainless steel pans

Dissolve 12 oz lye in 32 oz softened water in a plastic or glass bowl. Pour the lye slowly and in a steady stream, stirring constantly. Set aside to cool.

In a metal pot, melt 24 oz coconut oil and 38 oz solid vegetable shortening. Add 25 oz olive oil (not virgin) and any fragrance oils you want to use. Set this aside to cool, also.

Grease your soap mold with lard.
When both the oil and lye mixtures have cooled to room temperature, slowly combine them, adding the lye to the oils, stirring slowly and constantly.

Let the soap drizzle from your spoon into the pot every so often. When it keeps its shape momentarily before sinking into the rest of the mix, it's ready for you add your oatmeal, coloring, and scented oil.

Put some of the soap into a cup and stir in your extras, then put back into the pot.

Pour the soap into your mold.

Wrap the mold in a towel and leave it undisturbed for 24 hours. The soap mixture will heat up and then cool down. Avoid uncovering it until it's completely cooled.

Uncover and leave the soap to sit for another 12 hours, then turn the mold over and ease out the soap onto a clean surface.

Using a knife, cut the soap into bars.

Let the bars cure for four weeks before using.

You can vary the above basic recipe by exchanging butter for lard. Experiment with scents and textures. For example, use orange juice and peel, rose water and petals, oatmeal, cloves, ginger, or mint. Once you've mastered the technique, the sky's the limit as far as creating your own brand. Violets are the flower of Ireland, and a beautiful scent to add to your soap.

MIDSUMMER

Midsummer celebrations are always associated with bonfire customs. In Gaelic, Bonfire Night is known as *Oíche an Teine chanáimh* or *Teine Féil Eóin*. As with most Druidic celebrations, fertility was at the root of it. The midsummer bonfire was lit at sunset and watched right through until the next morning. The ashes and fire brought blessings to the crops.

The shape was always circular so that people could dance around it. The evening began with everyone walking sun-wise around the fire while praying. Feats of bravery were attempted, such as jumping over the fire.

Fires were lit from the bonfire around houses to ward off bad faeries, and communities had competitions to see who could build the biggest bonfire.

When growing up in Belfast, I remember wonderful bonfire nights on July 11th. We didn't walk sun-wise around the fire or even think about more than the fun we were having, but friends of all religions gathered around together to celebrate. We foolishly took turns jumping over it, and it was the one night of the summer our parents let us stay out very late.

SUNBURN

This time of year can also bring sunburn if you stay out too long without sunscreen. Buttermilk was used in the past to soothe sunburn when needed, but in the old days, peasants grew up in the fields, well weathered and used to the sun. Aristocrats would withdraw from the heat of the day, and only venture out with a parasol for protection. Nowadays, yogurt is much more effective, and easier to find. Yogurt smoothed over the burned areas will help relieve the smarting, red skin. Apply to affected areas and leave to dry, which takes about ten minutes. Gently remove with damp cotton-wool pads.

Yogurt is also a rich source of protein, vitamins A and D, plus riboflavin and calcium. It is easily digested, and recommended by doctors for relief of ulcers and an effective antacid. Eat yogurt to help reduce tension, fight insomnia, and when you are taking antibiotics, which kill off healthy bacteria in the intestines: yogurt recreates the necessary acid environment for the intestinal flora to flourish once more.

MAKING YOGURT

You need a starter - a teaspoon of fresh, unflavored yogurt. Use natural, organic yogurt for best results. Heat 1 pint of milk and remove from flame just as boiling point is reached. The milk must be cooled before the starter is introduced: yogurt bacteria live between temperatures of 30 C/90 F and 50 C/120 F. The perfect temperature for successful yogurt making is 45(C/115(F. To check the temperature, use a kitchen thermometer or dip your elbow into the milk; if it feels just above body temperature, the milk is ready to be mixed with the starter.

Add the milk gradually to the starter, stirring well. Do not be tempted to use too much starter as the yogurt will not be thicker, but lumpier. Pour into a container and cover. Organic yogurts tend to be runny, so you can stir in 4 teaspoons of skimmed milk powder before fermenting to thicken.

Incubate the mixture in either of the following ways: a wide-mouthed vacuum flask will keep the temperature constant; rinse in hot water first to warm it up. Wrap towels around the container and place somewhere warm where the mix will not be disturbed.

The yogurt usually takes eight hours to ferment; but it may take as little as five hours in a vacuum flask, or as long as twenty-four. Your yogurt has not failed if there is a watery separation on top; this is just whey, and can be drained off.

‖‖

HAZEL

COLL

August 6th – September 2nd

The HAZEL tree is known as the tree of wisdom. It was thought that if you ate the hazelnut, you'd gain magical skills and knowledge, and it was punishable by death to fell a hazel. If you are born under this sign you are artistic and creative, especially in the dramatic arts. You'll make an excellent teacher as you have a questioning and analytical mind.

The Sea God, MANANNAN MAC LIR, a master of disguise, rules this sign. He is a shapeshifter and a *psychopomp*, who guides safe passage for the newly deceased.

Your stone is the JASPER. This stone's elixir can be massaged into the temples to soothe troubled nerves.

The jasper promotes physical well-being, and can restore energy when flagging.

Your spirit animal is the SALMON, the oldest and wisest animal, which represents inspiration.

MERCURY is your planetary ruler.

STORYTELLING

In the summer months when the work is done, that was the time for storytelling around the fire. Many of these stories are passed down through generations, the source of the tale long forgotten. Here are a few of the more obscure Celtic tales that an elder might have held his family in rapt attention. My mother heard them from a nun teacher in Rosetta Primary School in Belfast, a mixed religion school.

THE COW THAT ATE THE PIPER

There were three spalpeens coming home to Kerry from Limerick one time after working there. On their way, they met a piper on the road. "I'll go along with ye," said the piper.

"All right," they said. The night was very cold, freezing hard, and they were going to perish. They saw a dead man on the road with a new pair of shoes on his feet.

"By heavens!" said the piper. "I haven't a stitch of shoes on me. Give me that spade to see if I can cut off his legs."

T'was the only way he could take off the shoes. They were held on by the frost. So he took hold of the spade and cut off the two feet at the ankles. He took them along with him. They got lodgings at a house where three cows were tied in the kitchen. "Keep away from that gray cow," said the servant girl, "or she'll eat your coats. Keep out from her."

They all went to sleep. The three spalpeens and the piper stretched down near the fire. The piper heated the shoes and the dead man's feet at the fire and got the shoes off. He put on the shoes and threw the feet near the gray cow's head. Early next morning he left the house wearing his new pair of shoes. When the servant girl got up, she looked at the door. It was bolted, and the three spalpeens were asleep near the fire.

"My God!" she cried. "There were four of ye last night, and now there are only three. Where did the other man go?"

"We don't know," they said. "How would we know where he went?"

She went to the gray cow's head and found the two feet. "Oh my!" she cried. "He was eaten by her." She called the man of the house. "The gray cow has eaten one of the men," said she.

"What's that you're saying?" asked the farmer. "I'm telling the truth," she said. "There's only his feet left. The rest of him is eaten."

The farmer got up. "There were four of ye there last night, men," said he. "There were," said one of the spalpeens, "and our comrade has been eaten by the cow."

"Don't cause any trouble about it," said the farmer. "Here's five pounds for ye. Eat your breakfast and be off. Don't say a word." They left when they had the breakfast eaten. And they met the piper some distance from the house, and he dancing on the road. Such a thing could happen!
(Anonymous - 10th century)

THE BEST AND WORST NAIL IN THE ARK

The shipwright who made the Ark left empty a place for a nail in it, because he was sure that he himself would not be taken into it. When Noah went into the Ark with his children as the angel had told him, Noah shut the windows of the Ark and raised his hand to bless it. Now the Devil had come into the Ark along with him and when Noah blessed the Ark, the Devil found no other way but the empty hole which the shipwright had left unclosed, and he went into it in the form of a snake; and because of the tightness of the hole he could not go out nor come back and he was like this until the Flood ebbed and that is the best and the worst nail that was in the Ark.

(16th century)

THE CAT AND THE DOG

Long ago the dog used to be out in the wet and the cold, while the cat remained inside near the fire. One day, when he was "drowned wet," the dog said to the cat, "You have a comfortable place, but you won't have it any longer. I'm going to find out whether I have to be outside every wet day, while you are inside."

The man of the house overheard the argument between the two and thought that it would be right to settle the matter. "Tomorrow," said he, "I will start a race between ye five miles from the house, and whichever of ye comes into the house first will have the right to stay inside from then on. The other can look after the place outside."

Next day, the two got themselves ready for the race. As they ran toward the house, the dog was a half-mile ahead of the cat. Then he met a beggar man. When the beggar man saw the dog running toward him with his mouth open, he thought he was running to bite him. He had a stick in his hand and he struck the dog as he ran by. The dog was hurt and started to bark at the beggar man and tried to bite him for satisfaction.

Meanwhile the cat ran toward the house, and she was licking herself near the fire and resting after the race when the dog arrived.

"Now," said the cat when the dog ran in, "the race is won, and I have the inside of the house for ever more."
(13th century)

THE FOX AND THE EAGLE

There came a very bad year one-time. One day the fox was near the shore of the Lakes of Killarney, and he couldn't find a bird or anything else to eat. Then he spied three ducks a bit out from the shore and thought to himself that if he could catch hold of them, he would have a fine meal. There was some water parsnip with very large leaves growing by the shore, and he swam out to it and cut off two big leaves of it with his teeth. He held one of them at each side of his mouth and swam toward the ducks. They never felt anything until he had taken one of them off with him. Very satisfied with himself, he brought her ashore, laid her down, and decided to try and catch the other two as well - 'tis seldom there would be an offer!

He caught a second duck by the same trick and left her dead near the first. Then out he swam for the third and brought her in. But, if he did, there was no trace of the other two where he had left them.

"May god help me!" said he. "I have only the one by my day's work. What'll I do? I wonder who is playing tricks on me." He looked all around but couldn't see an enemy anywhere.

Then he looked toward the cliff that was nearby, and what did he spy but the nest of an eagle high up on it. "No one ever took my two ducks but the eagle," said he. "As good as I am at thieving, there's a bigger thief above my head."

He didn't know how to get at the eagle. Then he saw a fire smoldering not far away, where men had been working at a quarry a few days before. They had a fire and it was still burning slowly under the surface of the ground. He dragged the duck to the fire and pulled her hither and thither through the embers. Then he left her down on the grass and hid.

The eagle must have been watching out for the third duck too, for down he swooped and snatched her up to his nest.

No sooner did the dead duck's body touch the dry nest than the nest caught fire---there were live embers stuck in the duck's feathers. Down fell the blazing nest with the three dead ducks as well as the eagle's three young ones inside it, so the fox had six birds for his supper.

Didn't he get his own back well on the eagle?
(10^h century)

VINE

MUINN

September 3rd – September 30th

The Vine needs care to survive in the cold Celtic climate, so it became a symbol of sacred knowledge. Vines trust their senses and rely on a strong inner self. If you're born under this sign you are authoritative and have high standards. You are vulnerable, self-critical, and very perceptive.

The Tuatha de Danaan, GODS OF LIGHT, rule this sign. They were one of the first pre-Christian peoples to invade Ireland

Your stone is the TIGER'S EYE. This stone's elixir can be massaged on the neck to soothe a sore throat, and on broken bones to aid healing. It helps bring clarity of thought, and is said to aid better eyesight in the dark.

Your spirit animal is the SWAN, which represents grace and beauty.

VENUS is your planetary ruler.

CELTIC RECIPES

Here are a few old-fashioned Irish recipes, straight from my mother's handwritten cookbook.

Potato Bread

1½ lb Potatoes
1 oz melted marg
4 oz. Flour
salt

Cook Potatoes. Mash; add salt & knead in marg. Mix in flour gradually until elastic consistency. Roll out ¼" cook slowly till brown on floured quddle.

SODA FARLS

3½ cups flour (either cake flour or all-purpose)
I teaspoon sugar
I teaspoon salt
I teaspoon bicarbonate of soda

Between 8-10 fluid ounces buttermilk to mix. Sift the dry ingredients together several times to make sure the bicarbonate is evenly distributed. Put in a large bowl and make a well in the center. Pour about three-quarters of the buttermilk in, and stir. lend until the dough becomes a ragged consistency. Then turn dough out onto a lightly floured breadboard, and to knead. When finished kneading, shape the bread. Flatten the dough into a circle, and place on a lightly dusted with flour baking sheet. Cut the circle into four wedges.

Bake in the oven for 45 minutes, the first 10 minutes at 450F, the rest at 400F. Dust a hot griddle or frying pan with a little flour, and place the farls on top. Leave about ½ inch to allow for expansion. Give them about twenty minutes on a slow heat on each side to brown. When finished, take the farls off the heat and wrap them in a light dishtowel, hot side down.

CRUSTY ROAST LAMB

I shoulder of lamb, 4 lb
I cup fresh breadcrumbs
pinch mixed herbs
2 tablespoon soft butter
I ½ lb potatoes, peeled, sliced

I large onion, diced
I large cooking apple, peeled, cored and sliced.
I0 oz chicken stock

Wipe the lamb over, and cut crisscross slits around the top. Mix together the breadcrumbs, herbs, butter, salt and pepper. Rub the mixture onto the top of the meat, pressing down well so that it sticks. Fill the bottom of the roasting pan with the vegetables and apple, mixing them and the seasoning well. Put the joint on top, then pour the stock into the pan, but not over the meat.

Cover loosely with a piece of foil and bake at 400 F for half an hour. Then lower the heat to 350F, and cook for a further 20-25 minutes to the pound. Take off the foil for the final half hour, and check that the vegetables are nearly cooked. Finish the cooking without the foil, to let the top get brown and crusty.

BEEF AND GUINNESS CASSEROLE

I ½ lb beef
6 oz lean bacon, cubed
I lb shallots or small onions
cloves garlic
2 beef stock cubes
I tablespoon sugar
salt and pepper
basil and parsley
I tablespoon butter
2 tablespoon flour
I tablespoon wine or cider vinegar

1 bottle of stout/Guinness

Sauté the beef and bacon in a little oil. Drain off the excess liquid. Remove the meat and set aside. Add the butter to the pan, and melt. Stir in the flour to make a roux. Gradually stir in the stout. Place the meat and the small onions (peeled) in a deep casserole dish, and season with the salt, pepper and herbs. Crush the garlic and add to the ingredients. Sprinkle the sugar on top, and pour in the sauce. Cover and place in the oven. Cook very gently for up to 3 hours at 300F. Check occasionally. If the casserole seems to be drying a little, you can add more stout. Remove from the oven and mix in the vinegar.

GINGERBREAD LOAF

6 oz flour
3 oz rice flour
2 oz butter
2 oz ground almonds
¼ lb raisins
2 oz candied peel
½ teaspoon ground ginger
½ teaspoon bread soda
2 oz treacle (by weight)
3 tablespoons sour milk or sour cream
1 egg

Sift flour with soda and ginger, mix with rice flour and rub in the butter. Stir in ground almonds, halved raisins and sliced peel. Mix treacle with milk or sour cream and well-beaten egg, and mix with the dry ingredients. Turn into a well-buttered pan and bake 1¼ hours in a moderate oven (375F).

TROUT IN HERB AND CREAM SAUCE
4 rainbow trout, gutted
300 ml cream
85g butter
mixture of herbs
Finely chopped parsley, chives, basil, watercress, etc.

Poach the fish in court-bouillon for 10-12 minutes. Lift out carefully: remove skin and eyes. Keep warm. Boil the cream until it reduces by half. Whisk in knobs of butter gradually. Finally, add in finely chopped herbs. Pour the sauce into a serving dish and arrange the fish on top. Serve at once, garnished with lemon slices.

CHAMP
4 lb potatoes
½ lb chopped scallions
10 fluid ounces milk
4 oz Butter
pepper

Champ is served piled high on the dish, with a well of melted butter in the center. It is eaten with a spoon from the outside, each spoonful being dipped in the well of melted butter. (Both my brothers insisted on pretending the pile of potatoes was a volcano and the melted butter lava!)

Peel potatoes and cook in boiling water. Simmer milk and scallions together for five minutes. Strain potatoes and mash thoroughly. Add hot milk, and the scallions, salt and pepper, and half the butter. The traditional implement used for pounding potatoes was a wooden masher, pestle-shaped, called a *beetle*.

> *"There was an old woman that lived in a lamp;*
> *she had no room to beetle her champ.*
> *She's up'd with her beetle and broke the lamp,*
> *and now she has room to beetle her champ."*
> *(Irish Traditional)*

IRISH STEW
I pound lean beef pieces
I pound carrots & parsnips
I pound onions
I pound potatoes
salt & pepper
beef stock

Place beef with stock in saucepan and add cold water to cover. Bring slowly to the boil and simmer for one hour. Add onions, potatoes, carrots and parsnips. Season. Continue cooking until vegetables are tender.

This stew was a family favorite - we always had it on Thursdays!

The Blythes: Lizzy, Maureen (Mum),
Ian, Steve, and James (Dad)

Dad graduating from
Queen's University, Belfast

IVY

GORT

October I^st — October 28th

IVY is said to protect against witchcraft and evil spells, which is why having it growing over the house became so popular. The clinging ivy by its nature is strong and determined. If you're born under this sign you'll also be strong and determined. You are cooperative, eager to please, and possess a lot of charisma. You win friends easily and are infectiously optimistic

The faery bride, GUINEVERE, rules this sign. Her name means *white shadow*, and she is also a May Queen.

Your stone is the SODALITE. This stone's elixir can be used to massage over the pancreatic and digestive areas when having problems. The stone helps prevent insomnia and helps keep you focused and logical.

Your spirit animal is the BUTTERFLY, represents faery faith.

PERSEPHONE is your planetary ruler.

FALL INTO WINTER

As Fall approaches Winter it is the time to start taking care of your skin and keep yourself looking and feeling your best through the cold months. I can only hope to look as good as my mother did at age 75. She believed in the restorative powers of facial massage and meditation.

FACE MASSAGE
This will tone up the underlying face muscles and improve the elasticity of your skin.

Cleanse your face thoroughly and wash your hands. Rinse your face with warm water and gently pat it dry. Dab some oil or cream on your fingers, and using the palms of your hands, stroke your forehead gently from one temple to another. Do the same from your chin up to your temples.

Stroke down from the corners of your jawbone to the neck and shoulders. Pat and stroke gently around the eyes, starting at the nose and sweeping out to the eyebrows. Repeat the first four movements more firmly, but don't drag the skin. Massage gently with your fingertips in a spiral movement over the same areas.

Where lines are beginning to form, very gently pinch the skin between thumb and forefinger, and press gradually at the same time with your middle and ring fingers. Gently beat against the same places with your fingertips.

Continue gently drumming the fingertips over your face. Slowly increase speed and pressure and then slow down again.

Here's one of my mother's favorite moisturizer recipes. She used this in her face massages.

ANTI-AGING MASSAGE CREAM
¾ oz white wax
¾ oz spermaceti
1¼ oz coconut oil
1¼ oz lanolin
2¼ oz sweet almond oil
3 drops tincture of benzoin

orange-flower water

Melt the fats and oils in a porcelain dish. Remove from the fire, add orange-flower water and benzoin. Beat briskly until creamy. Massage into the face and throat as described.

MEDITATION

Another way to fight the Winter blues is to learn how to relax and avoid letting a stressful life take hold. The following is a simple exercise in relaxation meditation.

Find a quiet place that makes you feel both comfortable and safe. If you've never meditated before, try different places until you find the best one for you.

Sit comfortably, with your back straight, not slumped. Let your eyes relax, and look down without focusing on anything in particular. Slow your breathing so that you are taking controlled, deep breaths.

Keep your eyes looking downward, and allow your mind to wander. If stressful thoughts interfere, take a deep breath and refocus your thoughts and concentrate on breathing.

Try and meditate for ten minutes every day. You'll soon notice a difference in your ability to cope with problems and stress.

MORE NATURAL BEAUTY REMEDIES

Cold cream is the first documented European recipe, from the Greek Galen, 2nd century AD. It makes an excellent base cream for all but the greasiest skin. Here are a couple of variations that worked for my mother.

ALMOND CREAM
12 tablespoons sweet almond oil
2 teaspoons rosewater
2 teaspoons butter
2 teaspoons grated castile soap

Melt the soap and oil together in a porcelain bowl laid in a saucepan. Gradually add the rosewater and butter while beating vigorously. Take from the heat but continue beating until the cream is cooled.

HONEY CREAM
I egg white
I tablespoon honey
I teaspoon almond oil

Beat the egg white until stiff, then gradually add the honey and oil. Keep beating until the mixture becomes smooth and creamy consistency. Leave on face for ten minutes, then rinse.

REED

NGETAL

October 29ᵗʰ – November 25ᵗʰ

The Druids believed the REED was a tree because of its dense root system. Reeds were used as pens, so came to represent learning and wisdom. If you're born under this sign you are independent, proud, meticulous yet complicated. You will not compromise, and are determined to make your own way in this life.

The Celtic God of the Underworld, PWYLL, rules this sign. A Welsh chieftain, he was Ruler of the Otherworld for a time, and honored for his conduct in a conflict with Arawen, King of the Underworld.

Your stone is predominantly the ROSE QUARTZ. This stone's elixir can be used in essential oils, for meditation. It is a balancing stone, bringing clarity to matters of the heart. It is a calming influence.

Your spirit animal is the HOUND. This was a title of honor for Celtic Chieftains as the Hound represented enduring loyalty.

Your planetary ruler is PLUTO.

SAMHAIN

This falls at the time of year when the earth has apparently died and everything is dormant. It celebrates the cycle of death and rebirth. Most cultures around the world believe that at this time the veil between our world and the Otherworld is fragile enough for us to communicate through it with our ancestors. October 31st has traditionally become a time to have fun with superstitions. Here are a few of my mother's favorite tales. She used to scare us silly making up stories about these at Halloween.

THE BANSHEE

Banshee or *Bean-sidhe* is Irish for faery woman. Her terrifying wailing is known as *keening*, which is from the Irish word meaning *lament*. She is harmless unless crying, which means someone is about to die. She is a pale figure with silver-gray hair streaming to the ground and a cloak of a cobweb texture clinging to her frail body. Her face is wan, her eyes red with never-ending crying. Banshees attend the funerals of the dead but are never seen, though sometimes her keening can be heard. She follows true Irish born across the ocean to distant lands wherever the true Irish have settled. But they never forget their blood ties; and neither does she.

SELKIES

These creatures are seals by day and human at night. In their human form, the Selkies possess an unearthly beauty, with dark hair and luminous, penetrating eyes. Silently they emerge from the sea to shed their skins and dance on the sand. It is said they must obey anyone who secures their oily skins. Female Selkies, caught in the nets of fishermen, make excellent wives. But they are solitary and quiet by nature, daily wandering to the shore to stare out longingly into the sea. If their fishermen-husbands are lost at sea in a storm, the Selkie will sing from the cliffs to guide them home. If a Selkie ever finds her seal skins again, she will inevitably be drawn back to the sea. She will never forget her husband and children, and stays close to the shore to watch over them.

LEPRECHAUNS

The Leprechaun is at heart a good faery, but with a wicked sense of humor and fun. He is a master cobbler and of leather work. Leprechauns guard the fairies' treasures and famous pot of gold. They must prevent it from falling into mortal hands. Although they hide the gold well, it is well known a rainbow's end indicates where the pot is buried. That's why you might be able to glimpse a Leprechaun when a rainbow is present; he's on alert to guard the gold! If a mortal managed to catch a Leprechaun, he or she can demand the gold or three wishes. It's always better to take the gold, for the wily Leprechaun will trick you whenever he can! "Nasty wee buggers," my mother called them, but she had a special place for them in her heart. She'd never tread on a ring of mushrooms, for example, or enter a faery ring of trees.

CHANGELINGS

When a mother finds a scrawny, ill-tempered, wrinkly little thing in the cradle, she knows instantly that the fairies have taken her child and left a Changeling. The dwarfed form and irritable manner passes for a child for a time, but soon it becomes obvious what has happened. Each Changeling has a distinctive personality like any human; but ugliness and an ill temper are generic traits. A family whose child is abducted may be fooled into thinking the Changeling is their own, and when the sickly dwarf sickens and dies, they sadly bury it and mourn, never realizing that their own child frolics happily in faeryland. Placing a set of bagpipes by the cradle is a sure test to discover whether the child is faery. No Changeling can resist them. Soon faery music spills out of the house and into the village, paralyzing with joy all those who hear the sounds. Boiling eggshells is another way of flushing out the interloper. A mother boils eggshells in front of the cradle. In an old man's cracked voice, the Changeling will cackle with laughter at the notion of making dinner from eggshells. To dispose of Changelings masking as mortals, there are two remedies. Heat a red-hot shovel, shovel the faery up and cast him onto a dunghill or into a chimney fire, or force foxglove tea down his throat and wait until it burns out his intestines. Once the Changeling is ousted, the original human child is miraculously returned.

FAERY ANIMALS

Many animals roam faeryland, and frequently stray into our realm. Magnificent horses have risen from the sea, only to be entangled in a fisherman's net. Cows often come from the sea in search of fresh, dewy grass. On May Day, it is said that faery cows appear and bring good luck to the farmer whose fields they cross. Black cats and lake serpents guard the faery treasure well. Cats, as legends have it, were once serpents and that is why they are so hard to kill and so dangerous to meddle with.

Faery animals can defy natural laws. Cows breathe under water; pigs appear and disappear at will. Trout and salmon converse with mortals in fluent Irish. Faery hares have been caught, washed, skinned and boiled, but never add a flavor to the soup; nor can a mortal sink his teeth in their flesh. A faery trout when thrown in a pan will not brown, and has been known to leap from the fire and out the door only to disappear.

THE BLARNEY STONE

A block of limestone known as the Blarney Stone is Ireland's lucky charm. Set in a tower of Blarney Castle in County Cork in 1446, the stone is reputed to have magical powers. Legend has it that an old woman cast a spell on a king as a reward for saving her life. Under this spell, if he kissed the stone he'd gain great powers of eloquence. Today people travel from all over the world to kiss the stone and gain the gift of gab. (I have kissed it twice!)

ELDER

RUIS

November 26ᵗʰ – December 22ⁿᵈ
WINTER SOLSTICE December 21ˢᵗ

The ELDER tree was sacred to the faeries. It was considered unlucky to burn elder wood, and bad luck to bring it indoors. If you're born under this sign you are impetuous and outspoken. You are restless and abhor routine. You like mental challenge but won't let others pressure you.

The crown goddess and Celtic tribal mother, CAILLEACH BEARA, rules this sign. She is a hag deity with boar tusks who turns to stone and is reborn.

Your stone is the SNOWFLAKE OBSIDIAN. This stone's elixir is great for burning in essential oils for meditation. It brings balance, purity, and helps focus the thoughts.

Your spirit animal is the RAVEN, which represents protection and health.

SATURN is your planetary ruler.

DECEMBER 23RD

This is the extra day, added to adjust the calendar. It's not ruled by any tree and remains a mystery. In Robert Graves' interpretation of the ancient song *The Song of Amergin*, he writes: "Who but I knows the secret of the unhewn dolmen?"

(As an aside note, I find it fascinating to learn that since this book was published, I was diagnosed with Grave's Disease, named after him. Perhaps I should have left the dolmen well alone! Who knows?)

THIRTEENTH MONTH
MORE CHARMS AND SUPERSTITIONS

A red haired woman is considered unlucky. She is said to be typically Irish but were nonetheless treated with great suspicion, and if a man met one as he was going to work he would certainly forget all about his labors and go home.

To cause love, keep a sprig of mint in your hand until the herb grows moist and warm, then take hold of the hand of the one you love, and they will follow you as long as your two hands close over the herb. No invocation is necessary; but silence must be kept between the two parties for ten minutes to give the charm time to work.

The first person seen by a cat that has wiped its face with its paws may be the first of a household to die.

When yawning, make the sign of the cross instantly over your mouth, or the evil spirit will make a rush down and take up his abode with you.

It is unlucky and a bad omen to carry fire out of a house where anyone is ill.

Never disturb the swallows, wherever they may build, and neither remove nor destroy their nests; for they are wise birds, and will mark your conduct either for punishment or favor.

If the palm of your hand itches you will be getting money; if the elbow itches, you will be changing beds.

It is unlucky to offer your left hand in salutation, for there is an old saying: 'A curse with the left hand to those we hate, but the right hand to those we honor.'

If a chair falls as a person rises, it is an unlucky omen.

By accident, if you find the back tooth of a horse, carry it about with you as long as you live, and you will never want for money; but it must be found by chance.

To breakfast by candlelight on Christmas morning is lucky.

If your ear itches and is red and hot, someone is speaking ill of you.

If you say good-bye to a friend on a bridge, you will never see each other again.

If a bee enters your home, it's a sign that you will soon have a visitor. If you kill the bee, you will have bad luck, or the visitor will be unpleasant.

It's bad luck to put a hat on a bed. If you make a bedspread, or a quilt, be sure to finish it or marriage will never come to you. Placing a bed facing north and south brings misfortune. You must get out of bed on the same side that you get in or you will have bad luck.

When making the bed, don't interrupt your work, or you will spend a restless night in it.

A bed changed on Friday will bring bad dreams. Any ship that sails on Friday will have bad luck. You should never start a trip on Friday or you will meet misfortune. Never start to make a garment on Friday unless you can finish it the same day.

Think of five or six names of boys or girls you might marry. As you twist the stem of an apple, recite the names until the stem comes off. You will marry the person whose name you were saying when the stem fell off.

To drop a fork means a man is coming to visit.

If your nose itches, someone is coming to see you. If it's the right nostril, the visitor will be a female, left nostril, male.

If you dream of death it's a sign of a birth, if you dream of birth, it's a sign of death. Dream of running: a sign of a big change in your life.

It's bad luck to pick up a coin if it's tails side up. Good luck comes if it's heads up.

It's bad luck to leave a house through a different door than the one used to come into it.

If you drop scissors, it means your lover is being unfaithful to you.

If you leave a rocking chair rocking when empty, it invites evil spirits to come into your house to sit in the rocking chair.

If you catch a falling leaf on the first day of autumn you will not catch a cold all winter.

All wishes on shooting stars come true.

Two people pull apart the dried breastbone of a chicken or turkey until it cracks and breaks, each one making a wish while doing so. The person who gets the long half of the wishbone will have his or her wish come true.

If you bite your tongue while eating, it is because you have recently told a lie.

If a woman sees a robin flying overhead on Valentine's Day, it means she will marry a sailor. If she sees a sparrow, she will marry a poor man and be very happy. If she sees a goldfinch, she will marry a millionaire.

If a single woman sleeps with a piece of wedding cake under her pillow, she will dream of her future husband.

You must hold your breath while going past a cemetery or you will breathe in the spirit of someone who has recently died.

If the left eye twitches there will soon be a death in the family. If a dead person's eyes are left open, he'll find someone to take with him.

A white moth inside the house or trying to enter the house means death.

A bride's veil protects her from evil spirits who are jealous of happy people.

If 13 people sit down at a table to eat, one of them will die before the year is over.

Knock three times on wood after mentioning good fortune so evil spirits won't ruin it.

A bird in the house is a sign of a death. If a robin flies into a room through a window, death will shortly follow.

Light candles on the night after November 1. One for each deceased relative should be placed in the window in the room where death occurred.

If a clock which has not been working suddenly chimes, there will be a death in the family. You will have bad luck if you do not stop the clock in the room where someone dies.

If the person buried lived a good life, flowers will grow on the grave. If the person was evil, weeds will grow.

A swan's feather, sewed into the husband's pillow, will ensure fidelity.

Bricks and mortar make a house, but laughter makes a home.

The believer is happy, the doubter is wise.

There is no need like the lack of a friend.

May you be in heaven a full half hour before the devil knows you are dead.

May your home always be too small to hold all of your friends.

And from me, an old and popular Irish saying that was my mother's favorite:

"May you always have work for your hands to do. May your pockets hold always a coin or two. May the sun shine bright on your window pane. May the rainbow be certain to follow each rain. May the hand of a friend always be near you. And may your god fill your heart with gladness to cheer you."

Cheers!

Lizzy

ABOUT THE AUTHOR

Lizzy Shannon is a multi-faceted bestselling author and editor. Born in Belfast, Northern Ireland, Lizzy is proud to celebrate her 10th birthday in 2012 as an American citizen. Most of the time she lives in Oregon, in between visiting family back in Northern Ireland.

Visit her website at: lizzyshannon.com

At the Legananny Dolmen, Northern Ireland

"Whatever genre Lizzy turns her hand to, you will not be able to put it down. A master storyteller."
- Thomas Nichols, Los Angeles Critics

"She writes in an uncomplicated, from the hip style. Great escapism."
- JC Andrijeski, Social Research, NY

"I LOVED this book almost instantly, because the reader immediately feels themselves the woman caught up in the plot."
- Amazon UK

"A fast-paced romp through an imaginative, wild world, inhabited with memorable characters and a fearless, fiery heroine. Strap yourself in for a thrilling trip."
- Ray Pitz, Editor, Sherwood Gazette

"Lizzy creates worlds that are both enticing and perilous at the same time."
- Paul Matera, Columbia West Inc

Read Time Twist by Lizzy Shannon

Caught in time... In the 21st century, humanity still believes they are alone in the universe. That changes. Temporal experiments from the future go wrong, and an innocent bystander, Catriona Logan, is suddenly thrust into a future where the Earth is a wasteland. Humanity now fights for the alien Leontors in a war against the reptoid Komodoans, in return for technology to re-terraform Earth. The war is at a stalemate. Catriona's unique 21st century brainwave patterns will ensure a victory to whoever can scan her first, and she becomes a pawn between the alien races. Captured, Catriona must unravel the threads of deceit and find a mysterious and compelling ally in a world where her rules no longer apply. Time is fractured and only Catriona can put it right, but at what cost?

Dragon Moon Press
- ISBN-10: 1897492006
- ISBN-13: 978-1897492000

CPSIA information can be obtained at www.ICGtesting.com
Printed in the USA
LVOW13s1930060614

388967LV00001B/25/P